Bank of Ireland.

A. Thom & C. Limited. Dublin.

Photo. Lafayette, Dublin.

THE
GREAT WAR
1914 - 1918

BANK OF IRELAND
STAFF

SERVICE RECORD
Compiled by THOMAS F. HENNESSY

Printed by
ALEX. THOM & CO. LIMITED. DUBLIN.
1920

F. ONEILL.

TO·OUR
HEROIC·DEAD
AND·TO·OUR
GALLANT·COLLEAGUES
WHO·FOUGHT
WITH·THEM

CONTENTS.

FOREWORD.

IT seemed to the Governors and Directors of the Bank of Ireland only right and fitting that this record should be compiled to perpetuate the memory of those members of the Bank who, in the dark days of the Great War, voluntarily came forward to fight for their country; ready, if need be, to make the great sacrifice for her sake.

Such men are not to be forgotten.

We welcome those who have come back to us. We mourn for those who shall return no more—

> " But trust that those we call the dead
> Are breathers of an ampler day
> For ever nobler ends."

G. F. S.

October, 1920.

PREFACE.

IN July, 1914, the male Staff of the Bank of Ireland numbered six hundred and twelve, about one-third of whom were over military age. Some of the officials were members of Volunteer Forces and a few were Army Reservists, but the great majority knew nothing of the art of War, and never expected that the time would come when they would be called upon to take up arms on behalf of their country.

At the outbreak of the great world struggle, the Board of the Bank determined that every possible effort should be made to release men for the new Armies in order to help in stemming the tide of the then unbeaten forces of the greatest military Power in the world. With this object in view, they made an Order granting half-pay, and a guarantee of reinstatement after the War, to all employees who volunteered. Lord Kitchener's call for men was issued about the same time, and was quickly responded to by the members of the Bank's Staff. So eager were men to join the colours, that in some instances, they left their posts in the Bank and enlisted, without acquainting those in authority, or waiting for formal permission to volunteer. The Board were thus faced with the problem of dis-

organisation of the Bank's business, and, to enable
the work to be carried on with an already depleted
staff, were obliged to suspend their Order, and
subsequent applications for permission to volunteer
were treated in rotation as circumstances permitted.

During the War period one hundred and ninety
Bank of Ireland men, or almost one-third of the
entire male Staff at the outbreak of the struggle,
served in the Forces. Of these, one hundred and
eighty-nine were volunteers, and only one was
called up under the Military Service Acts. It
must also be stated, in fairness to those concerned,
that, owing to the difficulty of making arrangements for carrying on the business of the Bank
during their absence, it was found impossible to
release many of the volunteers as early in the
struggle as they desired, and a further number were
obliged to remain at their posts in the Bank after
having expressed their willingness to serve.

Men of almost every rank in the Bank, from
Director to Porter, married and single, freely offered
their services, and, realising all that was at stake,
left their posts to engage in the great conflict.

The greater proportion of those who volunteered joined the ranks at the outset, but were
subsequently granted Commissions ; while, in
several cases, men who enlisted as Privates pre-
ferred to remain in the ranks. Many of the officials
attained high rank in the new Armies, and there is
an instance of a caretaker at one of the Branches

who enlisted, and was afterwards promoted to commissioned rank.

The Distinctions gained by Bank of Ireland men in the War number 40, and in several instances double honours have been won. An ex-official of the Bank, Sec. Lieut. Edmund de Wind, Royal Irish Rifles, who resigned the service prior to the War in order to emigrate, was awarded the Victoria Cross, but gave his life in performing the gallant deed which won for him the coveted distinction.

Forty-seven of those who joined the Forces were wounded, some of them severely—in one instance necessitating the loss of an arm, and in another, the loss of a leg.

Nine were taken prisoners—one by the Turks, and eight by the Germans.

Bank of Ireland men have served their country in the War on land, on sea, and in the air, with credit to themselves and to the Bank. They have served in places so widely separated as Russia and German East Africa, India and France, the North Sea and the Mediterranean. They have commanded batteries in Flanders, swept mines in the Adriatic, driven " caterpillars " in Mesopotamia, hunted submarines in the Channel, and fought duels in mid-air on several fronts. One of them, a Royal Irish Lancers reservist, fought with distinction " from Mons to Mons," and has survived the ordeal.

In the following pages will be found brief particulars of the services rendered to King and Country in the War by the members of the Bank's Staff. In many instances we are fortunately able to print extracts from letters received from Regimental Officers and comrades of those who fell, but in some cases it has not been possible to do this. We feel assured that this is not due to any want of appreciation of the services of the fallen, but to force of circumstances.

Happily a large number of those who served have returned to their peaceful duties in the Bank; and, while congratulations and thanks are extended to those who have come safely through the struggle, our gratitude is especially due to the thirty-three members of the Staff who will never return. Some were mere boys—all were true men. They little thought that the time would come when they would be acclaimed as heroes. War, with all its horrors and privations, its bloodshed and its sorrow, was utterly at variance with their very natures, but they went forth, cheerfully and willingly, to fight in a cause which they knew was just. They lie in France and Gallipoli, Belgium, Serbia and Egypt. They have raised to themselves a glorious monument in the triumph of the cause for which they fought; and the magnitude of their sacrifice on the altar of duty will ever be an inspiration to those who remain.

T. F. H.

ROLL OF HONOUR.

MEMORIAL TABLET.

Erected in Bank of Ireland, Dublin.

ROLL OF HONOUR.

MEMBERS OF THE STAFF KILLED IN ACTION,

DIED OF WOUNDS, Etc.

LANCE-CORPL. WILLIAM PERCY BUTLER

Royal Dublin Fusiliers

ELDEST SON OF W. J. BUTLER, ESQ., M.A., 36 York Road, Kingstown, Co. Dublin. Educated at Corrig School, Kingstown, and entered the service of the Bank in April, 1915. He enlisted in 10th Battalion Royal Dublin Fusiliers in February, 1916, and served during the rising in Dublin. He was sent to France in the following August, and after serving on various fronts, was mortally wounded by shell-fire in action at Gavrelle (supposed) on 23rd April, 1917, and died at No. 19 Casualty Clearing Station on the next day.

The following extracts have been taken from letters received by his parents, viz. :—

Platoon Commander : " Your son was a thoroughly reliable soldier, in whom his officers had every confidence, and his loss is much felt by his comrades in the Battalion, amongst whom he was most popular."

A comrade : " No man ever had a better chum— he was always the same—even under the most trying circumstances he never grumbled."

Photo by]   [C, Neville Cook, Kingstown.

LANCE-CORPORAL WILLIAM PERCY BUTLER,

Royal Dublin Fusiliers.

Photo by]   [F. W. D, Childerstone, Woking.

Lieut. William Ernest Albert Clayton,

Cheshire Regiment.

LIEUT. WILLIAM ERNEST ALBERT CLAYTON

Cheshire Regiment

SON OF REV. W. J. CLAYTON, The Manse, Warrenpoint. Educated at the Methodist College, Belfast, and entered the service of the Bank in June, 1907. Shortly after the outbreak of War he joined Queen's University O.T.C., and was commissioned in 11th Batt. Cheshire Regiment in December, 1914. He was sent to France in December, 1915, and was appointed Bombing Officer to the 9th Battalion. He was mortally wounded when on duty in support trenches near La Bassée on 13th April, 1916, and died from the effects nine days later, at the Casualty Clearing Station, Merville.

The following extracts have been taken from letters received by his relatives, viz. :—

Lieut.-Colonel : " He was one of my most valued Officers. Nothing he was asked to perform was too much for him, and his willingness and the energy with which he undertook any new duties were a splendid example to the other Officers and the men under him. He was universally loved and respected by the whole Battalion, and is a great loss to me personally, to the Battalion, and more especially to his Company, in which he had the greatest influence."

Captain : " He was quite the cheeriest fellow, and we miss him no end."

Lieutenant : " The loss to the Company is a great one. The men were very fond of him, and he was the very soul of cheerfulness, and life of the mess."

3

LIEUT. JOHN COLLEN

Royal Flying Corps

SON OF F. D. COLLEN, ESQ., Carricklee, Levaghery, Portadown. Educated at Campbell College, Belfast, and entered the service of the Bank in May, 1914. He enlisted in the 7th Batt. Leinster Regiment (Cadet Corps) in June, 1915, and was subsequently gazetted to a Commission in the 7th Batt. Royal Inniskilling Fusiliers. He was sent to France in February, 1916, and took part in actions at Loos and in the memorable gas attack at Hulloch. In August following he was transferred to the Royal Flying Corps, and qualifying for his badge in a short time, was attached to the 7th Squadron, and was principally employed as observer. He was engaged in this work, when his machine was brought down near Pys, about a mile on the German side of the lines, on the morning of 25th October, 1916. He was officially posted as " missing " on that date, and all efforts have failed to obtain definite information as to his fate.

The following extracts have been taken from letters received by his relatives, viz. :—

Major : " A keen and reliable observer, always ready to do his share of work."

Flight Commander : "I found him a very excellent and trustworthy officer; he was a favourite in the mess."

Captain : " I have had him up with me on several occasions, and have always found him most reliable and cool, and good at his work. I am sure he would have made a very good pilot if the luck had been his."

LIEUT. JOHN COLLEN,

Royal Flying Corps.

SECOND LIEUT. CHARLES FREDERICK CRAIG,

Royal Irish Rifles.

SEC. LIEUT. CHARLES FREDERICK CRAIG

Royal Irish Rifles.

SON OF JOHN CRAIG, ESQ., Kildare Street, Newry. Educated at Newry Intermediate School, and in Belfast, and entered the service of the Bank in April, 1911. He was commissioned in the 7th Batt. Royal Irish Rifles in October, 1915, and was subsequently attached to the 10th Batt. of the same Regiment. On being sent to France in June, 1916, he took part in the opening stages of the Somme offensive. After two days of severe fighting at Thiepval on 1st and 2nd July, 1916, his Battalion was relieved, he being the only surviving Officer of his Company. He was killed by a shell on the following day.

5

SEC. LIEUT. ARTHUR VIVIAN GREEN

Royal Dublin Fusiliers.

SON OF HERBERT P. GREEN, ESQ., Limehurst, Holland Park, Knock, Co. Down. Educated at the Methodist College, and Royal Academical Institution, Belfast, and entered the service of the Bank in July, 1913. He joined the Inns of Court O.T.C. in January, 1916, and was commissioned in the 5th Batt. Royal Dublin Fusiliers in December, 1916. Subsequently attached to the 8th Batt., he was sent to France in February, 1917, and took part in actions at Messines, Wytschaete, and the Ypres-Menin Road. He was killed near Ypres on 17th August, 1917, by shellfire whilst leading his platoon.

The following extracts have been taken from letters received by his relatives, viz. :—

Captain : " In all extremities he was the same genial and lion-hearted boy, and his men were absolutely devoted to him."

Lieutenant : " He was a fine Officer. He was deeply religious in his own quiet unassuming way—and this must have influenced for good many of those who knew and loved him."

Sec. Lieut. : " His character was one of the finest I have met with."

Chaplain : " We have still with us the sweet memory of his noble life and example."

6

Photo by]   [*Lafayette, Dublin.*

SECOND LIEUT. ARTHUR VIVIAN GREEN,

Royal Dublin Fusiliers.

SECOND LIEUT. FRANK DOUGLAS GUNNING,

Royal Inniskilling Fusiliers.

SEC. LIEUT. FRANK DOUGLAS GUNNING
Royal Inniskilling Fusiliers.

SON OF THE LATE SINCLAIR GUNNING, ESQ.,
Willoughby Place, Enniskillen. Educated at Por-
tora Royal School, Enniskillen, and entered the
service of the Bank in May, 1912. He enlisted
in the 7th Batt. Royal Dublin Fusiliers (Pals)
in September, 1914, and left England for active
service with the Mediterranean Forces in July,
1915. He took part in the landing at Suvla Bay,
Gallipoli, in the following August, and was subsequently invalided home with dysentery. After
recovery, he was commissioned in the 6th Batt.
Royal Inniskilling Fusiliers, and in June, 1916,
was sent to France to the 11th Battalion. On 1st
July, 1916, he led the "Enniskillen" platoon of
his Company in the opening stages of the Somme
offensive, and was officially reported "killed in
action" on that date.

The following extracts have been taken from letters
received by his relatives :—

Co. Commander : " He was a splendid Officer, and one
we were all proud of. He was a great favourite with
both officers and men, and the survivors of his
platoon speak in the highest terms of how he led
them across ' no man's land ' in the face of heavy
shell and machine-gun fire. We all miss him."

A returned Soldier : " A bullet took off one of
his fingers, and as he was binding it up, his
men begged him to go back to the dressing
station. He refused—' his place was with them,'
he said—and he went on until a shell ex-
tinguished his bright and noble spirit."

7

SEC. LIEUT. PERCIVAL MAXWELL HARTE MAXWELL

Connaught Rangers

Son of Samuel M. Harte Maxwell, Esq., Glen Albert, Roscrea, Co. Tipperary. Educated at Fermoy Grammar School, and entered the service of the Bank in June, 1905. He enlisted in the King's Own Dragoon Guards in September, 1914, and was subsequently commissioned in the Connaught Rangers. On being sent to France, he was attached to the Royal Irish Rifles and was killed in action at Armentieres on 10th April, 1916.

Second Lieut, Percival Maxwell Harte Maxwell,

Connaught Rangers.

SECOND LIEUT. CHARLES LENNOX HENRY,

Royal Irish Fusiliers.

SEC. LIEUT. CHARLES LENNOX HENRY

Royal Irish Fusiliers

YOUNGEST SON OF JAMES HENRY, ESQ., LL.B., 32 Belgrave Square, Rathmines, Co. Dublin. Educated at Wesley College, Dublin, and entered the service of the Bank in February, 1914. He enlisted in the 7th Batt. Royal Dublin Fusiliers (Pals) in September, 1914, and took part in the landing at Suvla Bay, the Serbian Retreat, and subsequent operations at Salonica. He was sent home to a Cadet Corps in July, 1916, and was gazetted to a Commission in the Royal Irish Fusiliers in January, 1917. He was afterwards sent to France, awarded a Parchment Certificate for gallantry, and was killed in action at Messines on 16th August, 1917.

The following extract has been taken from a letter received by his relatives :—

Colonel : " He was a magnificent type of Officer, and had been specially selected by me to lead his Company. He was loved by his men."

SEC. LIEUT. HENRY MAYNE HITCHINS

Royal Irish Rifles

SON OF HENRY HITCHINS, ESQ., 39 Sandycove Road, Kingstown, Co. Dublin. Educated at Chesterfield, Birr, King's Co., The High School, Dublin, and T.C.D., and entered the service of the Bank in April, 1901. He enlisted in the 7th Batt. Leinster Regiment in October, 1914, and was subsequently commissioned in the Royal Irish Rifles. On being sent to France in December, 1915, he was attached to a Trench Mortar Battery, and was killed in action near Vermeilles on 18th August, 1916.

The following extract has been taken from a letter received by his relatives, viz. :—

Senior Chaplain : " It is only a short time ago since he saved the life of an Officer who was bleeding to death from a wound. His coolness and resource under shell-fire was well known to us all, and we mourn one who was loved by all who knew him, and especially the men of his Battery."

SECOND LIEUT. HENRY MAYNE HITCHINS,

Royal Irish Rifles.

Photo by]   [Behan, Dublin.

SECOND LIEUT. (ACTING CAPTAIN) DAVID
NOEL KARNEY,

Royal Dublin Fusiliers.

SEC. LIEUT. (ACTG. CAPT.) DAVID NOEL KARNEY

Royal Dublin Fusiliers

ELDEST SON OF J. B. KARNEY, ESQ., 100 Leinster Road, Rathmines, Co. Dublin. Educated at Sir John Ivory's School, Edinboro', and entered the service of the Bank in May, 1907. He enlisted in the 7th Batt. Royal Dublin Fusiliers (Pals) in December, 1914, and left England for service with the Mediterranean Forces in July, 1915. He took part in the landing at Suvla Bay, and was wounded whilst on the Peninsula. After spending over a year in Hospital at Cairo, he was sent to Serbia, and took part in several engagements on the Struma. He subsequently contracted malaria, was invalided home in 1917, and on recovery joined the Cadet Corps at Moore Park. He was afterwards commissioned in the Royal Dublin Fusiliers, and was sent to France, where he took part in the capture of the Hindenburg Tunnel. He was appointed Acting Captain in January, 1918, and was awarded a Parchment Certificate for gallantry in the field. He was subsequently placed in command of a Company of the 2nd Batt. Royal Dublin Fusiliers, with orders to hold the position, and was killed in action on 21st March, 1918.

LIEUT. CECIL JOHN KENNY

Royal Irish Regiment

THIRD SON OF H. B. KENNY, ESQ., Clyduffe House, Roscrea, Co. Tipperary. Educated at the Grammar School, Tipperary, and entered the service of the Bank in July, 1913. He enlisted in the Royal Engineers, Motor Cyclist Despatch Rider, in December, 1914, and was commissioned in the 10th Batt. Royal Irish Regiment early in 1915. On completion of his training he was sent to France as Signal Officer to his Battalion, and was wounded in action in July, 1916. After recovery, he was attached to the 30th Batt. Machine Gun Corps, and after taking part in severe fighting on various fronts, he was killed in action by a German Sniper at Ham, near St. Quentin, on 24th March, 1918.

The following extracts have been taken from letters received by his relatives, viz. :—

Officers of C. Company : " He was universally loved by his brother officers and men, and we are very proud of his association. He died fighting in an endeavour to save his gun. For two days he had bluffed the Boche and held up their attack, persuading the infantry to hold the line with him. He could have got away, but scorned to do so without his gun."

Adjutant : " He was a perfect gentleman in the very best sense of the word, and a splendid Officer as well. He was one of those characters who are incapable of doing anything that is not straight, honest, and kind. He managed his guns marvellously."

Photo by]   [Werner and Son, Dublin.

LIEUT. CECIL JOHN KENNY,

Royal Irish Regiment.

LIEUT. JAMES ELKIN KERR,

Machine Gun Corps.

LIEUT. JAMES ELKIN KERR

Machine Gun Corps

SON OF MRS. J. McSWEENEY, Diamond, Carn-donagh, Co. Donegal. Entered the service of the Bank in April, 1911, and enlisted in the Royal Engineers as Motor Cyclist Despatch Rider in April, 1915. He was commissioned in the York-shire Regiment in June following, and was sub-sequently transferred to the Machine Gun Corps, and promoted Lieutenant. He was sent to France in April, 1916, and took part in severe fighting at Ypres, Loos, on the Somme and in Belgium. He was wounded in action at Ypres in May, 1916, and again at Guillemont in the following August, and was mortally wounded by shell-fire near Dunkirque on 10th September, 1917.

The following extracts have been taken from letters received by his relatives, viz. :—

Co. Commander : " He died as he lived—a gallant soldier."

Lieutenant : " His death was a great blow to us all, for he had attained great popularity both with officers and men. The Company has lost one of its most capable Officers."

Chaplain : " We all miss him a great deal—he was a good Officer and staunch friend."

SUB-LIEUT. CHARLES ALOYSIUS MARKEY

Royal Naval Volunteer Reserve

FOURTH SON OF THE LATE PATRICK MARKEY, ESQ.,
Hibernian Bank, Navan, and Mrs. Markey, 8
Terenure Park, Terenure, Co. Dublin. Educated
at Clongowes Wood College, and entered the
service of the Bank in May, 1912. He was commissioned in the Royal Naval Volunteer Reserve,
"Hood" Battalion, in June, 1915, and was sent
to Gallipoli in October following. After serving
during the evacuation, he was sent to France,
and took part in engagements at Beaumont Hamel
and was gassed at the capture of Beaucourt. He
was invalided home for a month to recuperate,
and on returning to France, took part in a forced
march, which aggravated his weak state of health.
He was then ordered into hospital at Le Touquet,
and was subsequently invalided home for six
months. At the expiration of that period he was
posted to Blandford for light duty. As his ill-
health continued, he was sent to a sanatorium,
and in August, 1919, was sent home, where he
died on 23rd January, 1920.

SUB–LIEUT. CHARLES ALOYSIUS MARKEY,

Royal Naval Volunteer Reserve.

PRIVATE MICHAEL MILLETT,

Leinster Regiment.

PRIVATE MICHAEL MILLETT

Leinster Regiment

ARMY Reservist, and was called up to the Leinster Regiment at the outbreak of War. After a short training, he was sent to France in September, 1914, with the original Expeditionary Force, and was killed in action on 20th October, 1914.

SEC. LIEUT. RICHARD MOORE

Royal Irish Fusiliers

HAD served twenty-one years in the Royal Irish
Rifles prior to the War, and joined the 11th
Battalion in July, 1915, and was sent to France
as Company Quarter-Master Sergeant. He was
promoted Regimental Quarter-Master Sergeant in
1916, and returned in that capacity to the Depot
at Clandeboye, Co. Down. In September, 1917,
he was gazetted a Temporary Second Lieutenant
from the O.T.C., Cambridge, and with that rank
joined the 2nd Garrison Battalion, Royal Irish
Fusiliers, at Berehaven. He was subsequently
transferred to Salonica, where he died of dysentery
on 29th October, 1918.

Photo by]   [*Reid Bros., Belfast.*

Second Lieut. Richard Moore,

Royal Irish Fusiliers.

PRIVATE WILLIAM GREGORY MORGAN,

Leinster Regiment.

PRIVATE WILLIAM GREGORY MORGAN

Leinster Regiment

SON OF A. W. MORGAN, ESQ., 93 Donore Terrace, South Circular Road, Dublin. Educated at Diocesan Schools, Molesworth Street, Dublin, and entered the service of the Bank in January, 1915. In April, 1915, he enlisted in the 7th Batt. Leinster Regiment (Cadet Corps), in which he became an efficient bomber. He was sent to France in December, 1915, and after seeing considerable service on the Arras and Somme fronts was killed in action at Guillemont on 3rd September, 1916.

PRIVATE CECIL WILLIAM MURRAY

Royal Dublin Fusiliers

SON OF MRS. B. J. MURRAY, 17B Dartmouth
Square, Dublin. Educated at Waterford, and
entered the service of the Bank in June, 1901.
He enlisted in the 7th Batt. Royal Dublin Fusiliers
(Pals) in September, 1914, and left England for
active service with the Mediterranean Forces in
July, 1915. He took part in the landing at
Suvla Bay, and was killed in action at Kis-lar-
Dagh, Gallipoli, on 16th August, 1915.

Photo by] [*Norman Dewar, Dublin.*

PRIVATE CECIL WILLIAM MURRAY,

Royal Dublin Fusiliers.

CORPORAL JOSEPH WILLIAM McCANN,

Royal Engineers.

CORPORAL JOSEPH WILLIAM McCANN

Royal Engineers

SON OF MRS. McCANN, Keatings Park, Rathcoole, Co. Dublin. Entered the service of the Bank in April, 1911, and enlisted in the Royal Engineers as Motor Cyclist Despatch Rider in September, 1914. He was attached to the Mediterranean Expeditionary Force, and died of dysentery on 23rd August, 1915.

CAPTAIN JOHN OLIVER McELROY

Manchester Regiment

THIRD SON OF THE LATE GEORGE McELROY, ESQ.,
of Cuilmore, Gurteen, Co. Sligo. Entered the
service of the Bank in July, 1900. He was
commissioned in the Manchester Regiment in
July, 1915, and was posted to the 18th Batt. in
France in May, 1917. He was wounded at
Courtrai in August, 1917, and was taken prisoner
by the Germans at Passchendaele in the following
December. After spending almost a year in
captivity, he was repatriated on 26th November,
1918, and whilst awaiting demobilisation, died on
5th March, 1919, at the Military Hospital, Grimsby,
from pneumonia following influenza.

CAPTAIN JOHN OLIVER McELROY,

Manchester Regiment.

TROOPER FRANCIS O'CONNELL,

South Irish Horse.

TROOPER FRANCIS O'CONNELL

South Irish Horse

SON OF RICHARD O'CONNELL, ESQ., Rathvin, Fethard, Co. Tipperary. Educated at St. Mary's College, Knockbeg, Carlow, and entered the service of the Bank in May, 1915. He enlisted in the South Irish Horse in May, 1916, and was sent to France in the following September. He served various periods of dismounted duty in the trenches, and was killed by the explosion of a mine when on mounted patrol duty at Rausart, south of Arras, on 19th March, 1917.

The following extracts have been taken from letters received by his relatives, viz. :—

Lieutenant : " His loss is very much felt by all : he was very popular, and had done very well while with us."

Comrade : " He and another cavalryman were on reconnaisance when their horses became entangled in wire laid by the Germans. This caused a mine to explode which killed him instantly, and his companion, who survived an hour. You have lost as fine a fellow as ever put foot in France, and I have lost a pal whom I felt was dearer to me than a brother."

PRIVATE THOMAS J. PARK

Northumberland Fusiliers

SON OF THE LATE THOMAS PARK, ESQ., of Limavady,
Co. Derry.   Rejoined his old Battalion—5th
Northumberland Fusiliers—in August, 1914, shortly
after the outbreak of War, and was soon afterwards sent to France.   He took part in much
severe fighting in that country, and was wounded
in the spine at Hill 60 in 1915.   He spent three
months in an hospital in England, and was then
transferred to Dublin, where he died as the result
of his wounds on 1st January, 1916.

PRIVATE THOMAS J. PARK,

Northumberland Fusiliers.

SECOND LIEUT. WALTER LOWRY PRENTICE,

Connaught Rangers.

SEC. LIEUT. WALTER LOWRY PRENTICE
Connaught Rangers

YOUNGEST SON OF THE LATE B. MAZIERE PRENTICE, ESQ., Agent, Bank of Ireland, Roscrea, Co. Tipperary. Educated at Castle School, Roscrea, and Avoca School, Blackrock, Co. Dublin, and entered the service of the Bank in November, 1910. He was commissioned in the 4th Batt. Connaught Rangers in November, 1915, went to France in the following May, and was attached to the 1st Batt. Royal Inniskilling Fusiliers. He was wounded in December, 1916, during the Somme movement, and invalided home. He returned to France in May, 1917, attached to the 2nd Batt. Leinster Regiment, and took part in actions at Messines and Passchendaele. He was mortally wounded on 31st July, 1917, whilst leading his platoon in the Passchendaele Battle, and died at No. 2 Canadian Clearing Station on 3rd August, 1917.

The following extracts have been taken from letters received by his relatives :—

Lieut.-Colonel : " He had only served with us for a short time, but all ranks had learned to esteem his high qualities as a leader, and his loss is sorely felt. He was a gallant Officer and a good one, but has died a soldier's death in a good cause. I shall miss him very much in the Battalion for he was one of our most promising officers.''

Lieutenant : " As for the men, they lost not only a gallant and efficient Officer, but also a great friend, as he took a very personal interest in their welfare and comfort. He was the first over the parapet of our trench with the leading platoon."

LANCE-CORPORAL MICHAEL FRANCIS QUIRKE

South Irish Horse

SON OF THE LATE EDMOND QUIRKE, ESQ., of Pallas, Donohill, Co. Tipperary. Educated at the Christian Brothers' Schools, Tipperary, and entered the service of the Bank in May, 1904. He enlisted in the South Irish Horse in January, 1915, and on being sent to France, was attached to the 7th Batt. Royal Irish Regiment, and promoted Lance-Corporal. After taking part in heavy fighting at various sectors, he was dangerously wounded on 17th December, 1917, and admitted into No. 5 General Hospital, Rouen, where he died on the following day, after having his right arm and left leg amputated.

Photo by]   [Knight, Limerick.

LANCE-CORPORAL MICHAEL FRANCIS QUIRKE,

South Irish Horse.

Photo by]   [Elliott & Fry, London.

SUB-LIEUT. RICHARD ARTHUR WYNNE ROBINSON,

Royal Naval Volunteer Reserve

SUB-LIEUT. RICHARD ARTHUR WYNNE ROBINSON

Royal Naval Volunteer Reserve

SON OF REV. A. C. ROBINSON, Ballymoney Rectory, Ballineen, Co. Cork. Educated at Cork, and Grammar School, Bandon, and entered the service of the Bank in May, 1904. In Oct., 1908, he married Clemena Mary Elizabeth, only child of the late George Peirce Ridley, M.D., Tullamore. He joined the Royal Naval Volunteer Reserve in August, 1915, and was commissioned in January following. He was sent to France in December, 1916, with the Drake Battalion, Royal Naval Division, and was mortally wounded in action near Albert on 5th February, 1917.

The following extracts have been taken from letters received by his relatives :—

Officer : He behaved magnificently : he was responsible for the carrying of ammunition up to the firing line of one of our Battalions—a most important thing—and it was work full of danger, but I know he worked absolutely regardless of his own personal safety. He is a great loss to the Battalion, because he was one of the most manly Officers we had, and we all loved him, and I know that he was very popular with his men."

Officer : " He was cheery to the last, like the splendid soldier he was."

SEC. LIEUT. THEOPHILUS WILLIAM SEALE

Royal Munster Fusiliers.

SON OF THE LATE RICHARD SEALE, ESQ., Clonmel, and of Mrs. M. L. Seale, Gleneden, Tipperary. Educated at the Methodist College, Belfast, and entered the service of the Bank in May, 1902. He enlisted in the South Irish Horse in September, 1914, and was subsequently promoted Corporal. In August, 1915, he was commissioned in the 7th Batt. Royal Munster Fusiliers, was sent to France, and had been only two days in the front line trenches, when he was killed at the Somme on 22nd August, 1916.

The following extract has been taken from a letter received by his relatives :—

Adjutant : " He was one of the best of our young Officers, and his loss will be greatly felt."

Second Lieut. Theophilus William Seale,

Royal Munster Fusiliers

SECOND LIEUT. WILLIAM NICHOLAS SHERIDAN,

Royal Irish Rifles.

SEC. LIEUT. WILLIAM NICHOLAS SHERIDAN

Royal Irish Rifles

ELDEST SON OF ROBERT SHERIDAN, ESQ., D.I., R.I.C., Banbridge. Educated at Omagh Academy and Foyle College, Londonderry, and entered the service of the Bank in April, 1912. He joined the Inns of Court O.T.C. in June, 1915, and was commissioned in the Royal Irish Rifles in October, 1915. He was subsequently transferred to a School of Instruction in Dublin, and was awarded a First-Class Certificate in Bombing. On completion of his course he was appointed Battalion Instructor, which position he held until his departure for France in July, 1916. He was killed in action by shell-fire on 1st September, 1916.

The following extracts have been taken from letters received by his relatives :—

Colonel : " We shall miss him very much indeed. Though he had been with us only a short time, he had done good work, and was an excellent Officer."

Officers of A. Company : " By his jovial manner and kindness of heart he had endeared himself to us all, and we mourn his loss very much."

Lieutenant : " His death will leave me missing one of my best comrades."

Sec. Lieutenant : " From what I have heard he lost his life in an effort to save one of his men, which I believe he succeeded in doing at the great cost of his own : and how can man die better ? "

SEC. LIEUT. THOMAS CHARLES STUART

Royal Flying Corps

SON OF SAMUEL STUART, ESQ., Beechgrove, Arklow, Co. Wicklow. Educated at Mountjoy School, Dublin, and entered the service of the Bank in April, 1914. He joined the Inns of Court O.T.C. in June, 1917, and in the following October transferred to the Royal Flying Corps. He trained at various Schools of Aeronautics in England, and was due for service in France when the signing of the Armistice concluded hostilities. He was then sent to Marske-by-the-Sea, Yorkshire, where he contracted influenza, followed by pneumonia, to which he succumbed on 12th December, 1918, at the Military Hospital, Redcar, Yorkshire.

SECOND LIEUT. THOMAS CHARLES STUART,

Royal Flying Corps.

SERGEANT RICHARD SEALY SWAN,

Royal Dublin Fusiliers.

SERGEANT RICHARD SEALY SWAN

Royal Dublin Fusiliers

SON OF THE LATE THOMAS SWAN, ESQ., and of MRS. E. F. SWAN, 3 Winslow Terrace, Terenure Road, Dublin. Educated at the High School, Dublin, and entered the service of the Bank in May, 1897. He enlisted in the 7th Batt. Royal Dublin Fusiliers (Pals) in September, 1914, and left England for active service with the Mediterranean Forces in July, 1915. He took part in the landing at Suvla Bay, Gallipoli, and subsequent severe fighting on the peninsula. He was afterwards promoted Sergeant, and was transferred with his Battalion to Salonica, where he was invalided with malaria, and died at No. 28 General Hospital, Salonica, on 15th August, 1916.

PRIVATE THOMAS ARTHUR SYMES

Royal Dublin Fusiliers

SON OF SANDHAM J. SYMES, ESQ., of Hill View, Tinahely, Co. Wicklow. Educated privately, and entered the service of the Bank in April, 1905. He enlisted in the 7th Batt. Royal Dublin Fusiliers (Pals) in September, 1914, and left England for active service with the Mediterranean Forces in July, 1915. He was one of the Reserves landed at Mudros prior to the landing at Suvla Bay, and contracted dysentery, from which he died on 18th August, 1915.

PRIVATE THOMAS ARTHUR SYMES,

Royal Dublin Fusiliers.

Photo by]   [*Lafayette, Dublin,*

SECOND LIEUT. PHILIP EYRE TENNANT,

Connaught Rangers

SEC. LIEUT. PHILIP EYRE TENNANT

Connaught Rangers

SON OF THE LATE JOHN TENNANT, ESQ., Parkstown, Thurles, Co. Tipperary. Educated at Multyfarnham, and entered the service of the Bank in October, 1898. He joined the Inns of Court O.T.C. in December, 1915, from which he was commissioned in the Connaught Rangers in March, 1917. He was sent to France in the following May, and was attached to the Leinster Regiment. He subsequently took part in action at Messines Ridge, and was killed by an explosive bullet at Shrewsbury Forest, near Ypres, on 31st July, 1917.

The following extract has been taken from a letter received by his relatives, viz. :—

Battalion Commander : "He was a gallant Officer at all times, and his Company Commander tells me that his gallantry was particularly conspicuous on the day of his death. He is a great loss to us, and we shall miss him very much."

SEC. LIEUT. RICHARD WILLIAM TOPP

Royal Inniskilling Fusiliers

ELDEST SON OF R. W. TOPP, ESQ., Agent, Bank of Ireland, Newry. Educated principally at The Grammar School, Galway—where he held a Scholarship—and entered the service of the Bank in July, 1915. He was commissioned in the 6th Batt. Royal Inniskilling Fusiliers in February, 1916, and in the following June was sent to France and attached to the 11th Battalion for the purpose of completing his course of instruction behind the lines. Owing to his efficiency, he was almost immediately transferred to the firing-line, and placed in charge of a platoon, which he led through Thiepval Wood in the Somme offensive on 1st July, 1916, but fell severely wounded by shell-fire on that date. He was officially reported " wounded " and subsequently " wounded and missing."

SECOND LIEUT. RICHARD WILLIAM TOPP,

Royal Inniskilling Fusiliers

TROOPER CLEMENT DOUGLAS TURNER,

North Irish Horse.

TROOPER CLEMENT DOUGLAS TURNER

North Irish Horse

SON OF THE LATE R. TURNER, ESQ., Earl Street, Longford, and of MRS. TURNER, 111 Ulsterville Avenue, Belfast. Educated at King's Hospital, Dublin, and entered the service of the Bank in April, 1915. He enlisted in the North Irish Horse in November, 1915, and was sent to France in the following October. After seeing considerable service he was killed in action at Ypres on 21st July, 1917, when endeavouring to help a comrade.

The following extracts have been taken from letters received by his relatives :—

Commanding Officer : "He was the youngest in his squadron, and a good boy."

Lieutenant : "His death cast a gloom over us all. He was beloved by all, and was killed instantaneously when going to help another."

Comrade : "He was one of the best—a brave boy. He died a glorious death, and you ought to be proud of him."

SEC. LIEUT. JAMES NORMAN WATSON

Royal Inniskilling Fusiliers

SON OF THE LATE JAMES A. WATSON, ESQ., and of
MRS. FRANCES WATSON, Avon Lodge, Armagh.
Educated at the Royal School, Armagh, and entered
the service of the Bank in November, 1911. He
was commissioned in the 3rd Batt. Royal Inniskilling Fusiliers in December, 1915, and was
attached to the 1st Battalion in France in July,
1916. He was gassed in action at Ypres Salient
on 9th August, 1916, from the effects of which he
died on the following day.

The following extract has been taken from a letter
received by his relatives :—

Commanding Officer : " He stayed at his post till
morning came, and danger of a following-up
attack by the Germans had passed, and by his
cheerfulness and fine example to the men kept
his platoon steady and confident. He managed
to walk to the dressing station about noon on
the 10th, but collapsed when he got there. I
wish to express to you our sorrow at the loss
of a good comrade and a fine soldier."

Photo by]   [*Jas. Glass*, Derry,

SECOND LIEUT. JAMES NORMAN WATSON,

Royal Inniskilling Fusiliers.

ROLL OF HONOUR.

MEMBERS OF THE STAFF WHO
ENLISTED FOR THE WAR.

JOHN ACHESON

JOINED Inns of Court O.T.C. in January, 1916, and was gazetted Sec. Lieut. Royal Garrison Artillery in following November. Sent to Salonika in January, 1917, and served in the Balkans with 43rd Siege Battery until February, 1918, when he transferred to R. F. Corps in Egypt. Appointed Lieutenant in May, and was wounded in June, 1918. Awarded "Order of the Nile, 4th Class."

HERBERT JAMES ADAMS

ENLISTED in 7th Batt. Royal Dublin Fusiliers in September, 1914, and took part in Suvla Bay landing in August, 1915, and subsequent operations at Gallipoli, being wounded in action at Chocolate Hill. After recovery, he served with the 10th Batt. Royal Dublin Fusiliers during the Rebellion, and was discharged "Unfit for further service" in May, 1916.

JOHN FENTON ALEXANDER

ENLISTED in Royal Army Service Corps, M. T. Section, in April, 1918, and served in England until demobilised.

JOHN SAMUEL CHRISTIAN ALLINGHAM

ENLISTED in Royal Irish Regiment in November, 1916, was sent to France in March, 1918, and transferred to 7/8 Inniskilling Fusiliers after the March Retreat. He took part in engagements at Locre, Neuve Eglise, Wervick, etc.

ROBIN CECIL ANDERSON

JOINED Inns of Court O.T.C. in November, 1915, and was commissioned in 5th Batt. Royal Dublin Fusiliers in December, 1916. He served with the 10th (Service) Batt. and 2nd Batt. R. D. Fusiliers in France in 1917, and took part in actions at Arras and Cambrai in that year. He was attached to the Indian Army in February, 1918, and served with the 1/98th Infantry and 1/22nd Punjabis on North-west Frontier until March, 1919.

GEORGE STUART APPLEYARD

ENLISTED in 7th Batt. Leinster Regiment in May, 1915, and was sent to France with 16th Irish Division in the following December. Served at La Bassée, Hulloch, etc., and was wounded in action in July, 1916. He was subsequently gazetted Sec. Lieut. in 2nd Batt. Leinster Regiment, and served at Hargicourt and on Menai front. He was wounded for the second time in the attack on Ledgenhem in October, 1918, and afterwards took part in the advance to the Rhine. He was later promoted Lieutenant.

ALBERT SWITZER ASHMORE

ENLISTED in Royal Engineers as Motor Despatch Rider in December, 1914, and took part in the landing at Suvla Bay in August, 1915. Sent to Serbia in December following, and served in Macedonia until June, 1917. Gazetted to a commission in 3rd Batt. Royal Inniskilling Fusiliers in January, 1918, was sent to France in the following March, and attached to the 1st Batt. of same Regiment. He was wounded at Ledgenhem in October, 1918, during the advance from Ypres.

AUBREY ATHERTON

COMMISSIONED in Royal Army Service Corps in July, 1915, and was subsequently posted to 11th Division at Suvla Bay, where he served until the evacuation, and afterwards in Egypt. Sent to France in July, 1916, and served in that country and in Flanders until demobilised. Promoted Captain in September, 1917, and mentioned in despatches.

ROBERT BAIRD

JOINED Artists Rifles (2/28th Batt. London Regt.) O.T.C. in June, 1918, and was transferred to 20th O.C. Battalion in October following. He was subsequently gazetted Sec. Lieut. County of London Regiment.

WILLIAM YOUNG BATEMAN

JOINED Inns of Court O.T.C. (Cavalry) in February, 1916, and was gazetted to R.H. and R.F. Artillery in January following. He was attached to the 15th Division in France in April, 1917, and took part in actions at Arras, Ypres and Passchendaele. Sent to Italy with the 7th Division subsequently, and took part in actions at Montello and Lower Piave, and Asiago Plateau in 1918. He was promoted Lieutenant in July, 1918, and returned to France in September following. Evacuated with bronchial pneumonia in October, 1918.

PERCY CHARLES BELL

ENLISTED in South Irish Horse in September, 1914, and served in France from December, 1914, until December, 1916, when he was sent home and commissioned in the Royal Field Artillery. He was again sent to France in May, 1917, was awarded the Military Cross in March, 1918, was wounded in action, and subsequently promoted Lieutenant. Awarded M.C. " for gallantry and devotion to duty in the field. It was mainly due to his wonderful gallantry and cool organisation under intense hostile artillery and machine gun fire that his guns were successfully withdrawn. He has always shown exceptional keenness and devotion to duty worthy of the highest traditions of the Regiment."

ROWAN NETTERFIELD BERRY

ENLISTED in South Irish Horse in February, 1917, and transferred to Cavalry Officers' Cadet School, Kildare, in September following. Gazetted 2nd Lieut. 1st Reserve Cavalry Regiment (Lancers) in January, 1918.

GERALD O'HAGAN BEVERIDGE

CALLED up at outbreak of War, he joined his Regiment—the South Irish Horse—on 5th August, 1914, and was soon afterwards attached to the 49th West Riding Division. In April, 1915, this formation was sent to France, and took part in numerous actions, *i.e.*, Festubert, Ypres, Passchendaele, Cambrai, etc. In October, 1916, he was transferred to the Military Mounted Police, and promoted Sergeant-Major, with which rank he served until demobilised. He was awarded the Meritorious Service and Good Conduct Medals.

THOMAS BIBBY

ENLISTED in Royal Army Service Corps, M. T. Section, in July, 1916, and was subsequently appointed to the Examining Staff, and promoted Sergeant.

PATRICK BOLGER

ARMY Reservist. Called up at the outbreak of War, he saw considerable service with the Royal Army Service Corps in France, where he was wounded and gassed in action.

ALFRED BOWDEN

ENLISTED in 3rd Batt. Sherwood Foresters in May, 1918. Was subsequently sent to France, and took part in actions at Le Cateau, Selle River, and Landrecies in the advance of 1918.

JOHN HENRY TILSON BRABAZON

COMMISSIONED in 4th Batt. Connaught Rangers in September, 1914, and was sent to France in following April and wounded in action. After recovery he was sent to Mesopotamia, was again wounded and taken prisoner by the Turks in 1916, and was released after the Armistice.

ALFRED EDWARD BRAMBELL

JOINED Royal Engineers, as Motor Despatch Rider, in April, 1918, was sent to France in the following October, and attached to the 1st Corps Heavy Artillery in Belgium, with which he served until demobilised.

EDWARD JOHNSTON BRETT

JOINED 18th Batt. Royal Irish Rifles in June, 1915, and was commissioned in Special Reserve (3rd Batt. Leinster Regt.) in July following. Seconded to Machine Gun Corps in September, 1916, and posted to 18th Division in November, 1916. Took part in 3rd Battle of Ypres, Passchendaele offensive, March, 1918, and subsequent actions at Morlancourt, Trones Wood, Le Cateau, etc. Promoted Lieut. in February, 1917, and Captain in April, 1918. Mentioned in despatches, and awarded Military Cross : " For conspicuous gallantry and devotion to duty. During the absence of his Company Commander he commanded his Company with great dash and skill. He made many bold reconnaissances under heavy enemy rifle and machine gun fire which enabled the guns of the Company to secure positions from where they inflicted severe casualties on the enemy. On one occasion he pushed forward in front of our infantry and observed some enemy limbers pulling out. He succeeded in getting two of his guns on to them, and knocked out the enemy team. Throughout the operations his gallantry was beyond all praise, and he set an excellent example of courage and devotion to duty under fire to all ranks. He at all times proved himself to be a very cool and efficient officer and skilful leader."

JOHN FREDERICK WILLIAM BROWN

ENLISTED in 7th Batt. Royal Dublin Fusiliers in September, 1914, and took part in the landing at Suvla Bay in August, 1915, and was slightly wounded. He was subsequently promoted Lance-Corporal, and served in Serbia and Macedonia. Invalided to Malta in 1916, he was found unfit for further general service, and was transferred to the Garrison until demobilised.

ERNEST ALEXANDER BURD

ENLISTED in 7th Batt. Leinster Regiment in July, 1915, and was sent to France in the following December, and served at La Bassée, Loos, and on the Somme. Took part in the storming of Guillemont on 3rd September, 1916, and was severely wounded at Ginchy six days later. Discharged from the Army in May, 1917, owing to partial disablement, caused by wounds.

ALEXANDER BURKE

ENLISTED in 7th Batt. Royal Dublin Fusiliers in September, 1914, and took part in operations at Gallipoli in 1915. Transferred to 9th Battalion in January, 1916, and was wounded at the Somme in following September. He afterwards transferred to the Royal Air Force, and was attached to the 35th Squadron at Vendome and Nieuport for bombing and artillery observation.

JOHN WHITMORE BURLAND

ENLISTED in 10th Batt. Royal Dublin Fusiliers in May, 1916, was sent to France in the following August, and took part in actions at Lens, River Ancre, and Beaumont Hamel. He was invalided with shell-shock in November, 1916, and was discharged from the Army in May, 1917.

HERBERT MARSHALL BUTLER

ENLISTED in South Irish Horse in August, 1914, and was commissioned in 12th Batt. Manchester Regiment in the following November. He was sent to France in July, 1915, and took part in engagements at Ypres, Loos, Arras, and on the Somme. Appointed to a Regular Commission in the Indian Army in November, 1917.

WILLIAM ALFRED CAMPBELL

ENLISTED in 18th Batt. London Irish Rifles in May, 1918, and was sent to France in the following October. Took part in the entry of the British Troops into Lille after the German withdrawal, and subsequently served with the Army of Occupation.

EDWARD WILLIAM CARRETTE

ENLISTED in Royal Army Service Corps, M. T. Section, in September, 1917, and served in Mesopotamia, Egypt and Palestine, having driven a " Caterpillar " for various batteries of Artillery. Took part in the actions leading to the final defeat of the Turks.

JAMES JOSEPH CARROLL

JOINED Cadet Wing, R.F.C., in March, 1917, and was gazetted Sec. Lieutenant in June and Flying Officer in November following. He was sent to France as a Scout Pilot, and took part in the Cambrai offensive in March, 1918, and counter-offensive in August and September following. Promoted Lieutenant in April, 1918, and was twice shot down. Discharged unfit for further flying in December, 1918.

GEORGE UNIACKE CASHEL

JOINED Cadet Corps in 1916, and was gazetted Sec. Lieut., Royal Field Artillery, in the following year. He was sent to France in the Spring of 1918, was attached to the 31st Heavy Battery, Royal Garrison Artillery, then in the Arras Sector, and took part in the 1918 offensive, including the capture of Bourlon Wood, and Cambrai. Awarded Military Cross :—
" For conspicuous gallantry and devotion to duty in the field. The enemy put a heavy concentration of gas and high explosives on the Battery position, and six boxes of cartridges were ignited. With two N.C.O.'s, Lieut. Cashel rushed out, and, regardless of shell-fire, managed to extinguish the fire with earth and water, preventing the spreading and serious loss of stores."

REGINALD JAMES CONNOR

GAZETTED Sec. Lieut., Royal Army Service Corps, in September, 1914, promoted Lieutenant in the following March, and Captain in August, 1915. Transferred to the Infantry in September, 1916, and continued to serve in France until demobilised.

HENRY WYNNE CONWAY

ENLISTED in South Irish Horse in October, 1915, and was subsequently gazetted to a Commission in 4th Batt. Royal Irish Regiment. Sent to France in December, 1916, and took part in the battles of Messines and Wytschaete in June, 1917, being gassed at the latter engagement. Invalided home in July, 1917, and placed on retired list owing to ill-health, contracted on active service.

AUSTIN OWEN COOPER

COMMISSIONED in 11th Batt. South Staffordshire Regiment in March, 1915, sent to France in May, 1916, and served with the 41st Division on the Somme. Wounded in September following, he was sent home, and after recovery was promoted Lieutenant. He was again sent to France in November, 1917, attached to the 14th (Light) Division, and served as Captain with the 5th Army during the retreat on the Somme in March, 1918. Taken prisoner in May, 1918, during the German attack on the Chemin des Dames, and repatriated after the Armistice.

THOMAS JOSEPH COOPER

JOINED Dublin University O.T.C. in April, 1918, and subsequently transferred to Cadet School at Fermoy. Contracted double pneumonia, following influenza, and was certified unfit for further service.

RICHARD WILLIAM COURTNEY

ARMY Reservist. Called up at the outbreak of War, and joined the Royal Field Artillery. He took part in the retirement from Mons, the advance from the Marne to the Aisne in 1914, and in actions at Givenchy, Neuve Chapelle, Hulloch and Loos in 1915, and at Vimy Ridge and the Somme in 1916. Sent home with shell-shock in 1917, and on recovery was again sent to France, and served in operations at Passchendaele and Bullicourt in 1918, the retirement from St. Quentin to Amiens and the advance from Amiens to St. Quentin. Mentioned in despatches, and recommended for D.C.M.

ARTHUR CROSBIE

GAZETTED to a Commission in Cork Royal Garrison Artillery in June, 1915. Appointed Acting-Garrison Adjutant, Queenstown Harbour, in August, 1915, and promoted Lieutenant in July, 1917.

OLIVER CROSBIE

COMMISSIONED in the 4th Batt. Royal Irish Regt. in May, 1915. Sent to France in April, 1916, and was wounded at Loos in August following. He returned to France in December, 1916, was attached to the 2nd Batt. Royal Irish Regiment, and promoted Lieutenant in July, 1917. He took part in the battles of Messines and Amiens, and was again wounded at Bapaume in 1918.

JAMES ROBERT ROWLAND CUSACK

COMMISSIONED in the Royal Army Service Corps in April, 1915, promoted Captain in the following May, and appointed Adjutant of No. 1 Motor Transport Reserve Depot. In August, 1917, he was sent to France to organise Motor Transport from Cherbourg to Taranto, and in the following October was promoted Major, and employed with Italian units during the retreat. Subsequently attached to the French Army, and mentioned in despatches. In July, 1918, appointed " Deputy Assistant Director of Transport " on Staff.

ALAN VICTOR DAGG

ENLISTED in 6th Batt. Black Watch in September, 1914, and was later commissioned in the Leicester-shire Regiment. Saw considerable service in France, was twice wounded, and received special mention for capturing a German flag in an engagement.

LIONEL STANLEY DAGG

JOINED Cadet Corps, 7th Leinster Regiment, in April, 1915, was sent to France in following December, and served at Hulloch and La Bassée. Invalided with gas-poisoning and pleurisy in June, 1916, was later commissioned in King's Royal Rifle Corps, and joined the 9th Batt. at Arras in the following April, and served at Messines, Ypres and Passchendaele. Taken prisoner on 21st March, 1918, and placed in Lahr Camp until repatriated after the Armistice. Subsequently served at Cologne with Army of Occupation.

PATRICK DALLAS DALLAGHAN

ENLISTED in Royal Air Force, Cadet Brigade, in August, 1918.

EDMUND NOEL DEVITT

ENLISTED in Royal Army Service Corps in May, 1915, and was sent to France in the following month. Promoted Corporal in April, 1917, returned to England in February, 1918, and was commissioned Sec. Lieutenant.

JAMES MICHAEL DIVER

COMMISSIONED Paymaster Sub-Lieut. Royal Naval Reserve, in October, 1915, and served on Staff of Wing Captain commanding Royal Naval Air Service, Dardanelles, until after the evacuation in January, 1916. He later served as Assistant Paymaster, H.M.S. "Ark Royal," until April, 1918, and was subsequently appointed Secretary to Senior Naval Officer, Bristol Channel. Promoted Paymaster Lieut. with seniority, 30th October, 1917, and in New Year Honours, 1919, was awarded M.B.E. (Military Division) :—" In recognition of valuable services rendered in connection with the War."

EDWARD DONOHOE

ARMY Reservist. Called up at outbreak of War to Royal Irish Fusiliers, and was later transferred to Military Provost Staff Corps, and placed in charge of the Workshop, Cork Detention Barracks.

JAMES HENRY DORRITTY

ENLISTED in Royal Irish Fusiliers in August, 1914, and took part in the landing at Suvla Bay in August, 1915, and was wounded at Chocolate Hill. He was later promoted Sergeant and served in the Struma Valley operations in 1916, and on the Doiran front in 1917, being again wounded and losing a finger in the attack on Grand Coronne. Subsequently sent with G.H.Q. to Constantinople, acted as escort to the King's Messenger, and was promoted Company Quartermaster-Sergeant, and awarded the Meritorious Service Medal.

ALBERT LEO DUFFY

COMMISSIONED in Royal Naval Volunteer Reserve in December, 1917, and was attached to 4th Flotilla of Destroyers at Plymouth. His vessel served in three engagements with enemy submarines (two of which are known to have been destroyed) and accompanied the last convoy from America.

JAMES INGLIS EADIE

ENLISTED in 12th Royal Inniskilling Fusiliers in March, 1916, and was gazetted Sec. Lieut. in 3rd Battalion in March, 1917. Attached to Machine Gun Corps in May, 1918, sent to France in September, and was wounded in action in October, 1918. Subsequently served in Constantinople as Assistant D.A.P.M., and later was attached to Allied Police Control. Afterwards was appointed A.M.L.O. at Chanak with rank of Staff Captain, and served as a member of the Standing Military Court at Ismid for the control of rebel nationalists of Anatolia.

WILLIAM EGAN

ENLISTED in South Irish Horse in July, 1916, was sent to France in the following December, and served on St. Quentin front. Subsequently invalided with shell-shock.

WILLIAM RALPH EGAN

COMMISSIONED in Royal Irish Fusiliers in September, 1914, and was wounded at the Suvla Bay landing in August, 1915. Was afterwards attached to Army Printing and Stationery Services in France, and was promoted Captain, and subsequently Major and Deputy Assistant Director of A.P. & S.S. for Egypt, Palestine, and Constantinople.

JOHN JOSEPH FITZSIMON

ENLISTED in Royal Air Force in October, 1918, and was released after Armistice.

WILLIAM NELSON FOSTER

GAZETTED Lieutenant, Royal Army Service Corps, in August, 1915, and was posted to Main Supply Depot, Port Said, in January, 1916. Promoted Captain in September, 1916 ; appointed O.C., Main Supply Depot, Kantara, in February, 1917, and Major in following April. Later appointed O.C., Base Supply Depot and R.A.S. Corps, Port Said, and subsequently served as O.C., Supply Depots at Ludd, Palestine, Rayak and Beyrout. Three times mentioned in despatches, and awarded D.S.O. for organisation of Main Supply Depot, Kantara.

GEORGE HENRY FRAZER

AT outbreak of War, was recommended for a Commission, but was rejected owing to defective eyesight. Enlisted in R.A.M. Corps in September, 1914, and was attached to 58th Field Ambulance, 19th Division, on Salisbury Plain. Sent to France in July, 1915, and after the first Battle of the Somme was promoted Sergeant, and awarded the Military Medal for gallantry in the field, at the Battle of Messines, in June, 1917. Admitted to hospital suffering from mustard gas burns received in Cambrai sector in February, 1918, and on discharge, returned to original unit. Took part in all the operations of the 19th Division with the exception of the March, 1918, retreat.

GEORGE WARREN FRAZER

GAZETTED to a Commission in Royal Army Service Corps in April, 1915, and attached to No. 1 Base Supply Depot, Liverpool. Promoted Captain in following August, and Adjutant in February, 1916. Attached to No. 3 Base Supply Depot, Manchester, in May, 1916, and promoted Major in June, 1917. In December, 1917, appointed Officer in Charge of Shipping at King's Lynn and Boston, and in October, 1918, at Grimsby, Immingham and Hull. Awarded O.B.E. (Military Division) in King's Birthday Honours, 1919.

JAMES HERBERT GIBSON

ENLISTED in North Irish Horse in July, 1915, and served in France in 1916, and was promoted Sergeant. Subsequently commissioned in 7th Hussars, and saw considerable service in Mesopotamia, Persia, and in Russia. Promoted Lieutenant in February, 1919.

JOHN STRATTON GIBSON

ENLISTED in 15th Batt. Royal Irish Rifles in September, 1914; promoted Sergeant in following February, and transferred to the King's African Rifles for service in East Africa in May, 1917. Promoted Acting Regimental Sergeant-Major in June, 1918, and was mentioned in Lieut.-General Van Deventer's despatches.

JOHN WILLIAM GIFFORD

ENLISTED in 7th Batt. Leinster Regiment in May, 1915; was sent to France with the 16th Division in the following December. Served at Loos, Hulloch and Vermeilles, and awarded Parchment Certificate for raiding operations. Took part in actions at Guillemont and Ginchy in the Somme Battle of 1916, was subsequently promoted Sergeant, and served in Palestine in the successful operations against the Turks.

CECIL HERBERT GILLIGAN

JOINED Dublin University O.T. Corps in April, 1915, and was subsequently commissioned in 4th Batt. Royal Irish Fusiliers, with which Battalion he served in France, and later with the Tank Corps. Transferred to Indian Army in January, 1918.

MATTHEW CHARLES GILMORE

JOINED Cadet Corps, 18th Royal Irish Rifles, in April, 1916, and was commissioned Sec. Lieut. in August, 1917. Saw considerable service in France, and afterwards with the Army of Occupation.

THOMAS ALBERT GLANVILLE

COMMISSIONED in 3rd Batt. Royal Dublin Fusiliers in August, 1915, and was attached to 9th Batt. Royal Irish Rifles in France in July, 1916. Later attached to 107th Trench Mortar Battery, was wounded in October, 1916, and after recovery was promoted Lieut. in July, 1917. Served as Adjutant 3rd Royal Dublin Fusiliers, and with 1/6th King's African Rifles from November, 1917.

JOHN GOOD

JOINED Inns of Court O.T.C. in May, 1917, and was transferred to No. 2 Cavalry Cadet School in following April. Subsequently gazetted to 2nd Reserve Cavalry (Hussars), serving at the Curragh.

WILFRED CLOUGH AFFLECK GRAVES

ENLISTED in Royal Army Service Corps, M. T. Section, in January, 1917, and after serving in England, was discharged from the Army owing to ill-health.

EDWARD RICHARD GRAY

ENLISTED in 7th Royal Dublin Fusiliers (Pals) in September, 1914, and took part in the landing at Suvla Bay in August, 1915, and subsequent operations at Gallipoli. Later served at Salonica, and was wounded at Yenekoi in October, 1916. Commissioned in 3rd Batt. Royal Dublin Fusiliers in August, 1917, took part in the battle of Cambrai in November following, and was awarded Parchment Certificate for gallantry. Was wounded in the retirement of March, 1918, and was later transferred to England owing to breakdown in health. Promoted Lieutenant in February, 1919.

ROBERT GERALD GRAY

COMMISSIONED in Royal Army Service Corps in May, 1915, and posted to 16th Divisional Train. Sent to France in February, 1916; promoted Lieutenant in 1917, and subsequently transferred to the Tank Corps.

LIONEL FREDERICK GREEN

ENLISTED in 3rd Batt. Royal Irish Rifles in September, 1914, and was sent to France with 2nd Battalion in January, 1915. Invalided through illness in following April, returned to France in December, 1916, and took part in the battle of Cambrai. In November, 1917, was appointed Intelligence N.C.O., and served at the battle of St. Quentin. In May, 1918, he was sent home to train for a Commission.

FREDERICK WILLIAM HALL

ENLISTED in Royal Engineers, Motor Despatch Rider, in May, 1915. Sent to France in January, 1916, attached to Royal Artillery, and was mentioned in despatches for work at the battle of the Somme. Subsequently served at Arras, St. Quentin, and Passchendaele, and was severely injured in a collision with a motor lorry in December, 1917.

WILLIAM VERE HARLEY

ENLISTED in Royal Field Artillery in June, 1917; was sent to France in following February, and took part in the retreat of March, 1918. Invalided home with pneumonia and crushed foot in May, 1918.

DAVID WALTER HARRIS

JOINED Dublin University O.T. Corps in November, 1916, and was subsequently commissioned in the Royal Dublin Fusiliers. Sent to France in October, 1917 ; transferred to Royal Air Force in August, 1918, and was gazetted Observer in November, 1918.

CHARLES DACRE HARVEY

ENLISTED in 7th Batt. Royal Dublin Fusiliers (Pals) in September, 1914, and was soon commissioned Sec. Lieut. " A " Company. Wounded in the landing at Suvla Bay in August, 1915, and again in Serbia. Subsequently promoted Staff Captain, 29th Infantry Brigade, and was mentioned in despatches and awarded Order of the Nile, 4th Class. Later appointed to the position of Paymaster in Palestine.

SAMUEL HEGAN.

ENLISTED in Royal Air Force in June, 1918, and graduated as Flight Cadet.

CHARLES EDWARD HENNING

JOINED Inns of Court O.T.C. in April, 1917, and was gazetted Sec. Lieut., London Irish Rifles, in November following. Sent to France in January, 1918, and served in the Somme district and at Cambrai. Severely wounded and taken prisoner on 23rd March, 1918, and was repatriated after the Armistice.

GEORGE HENRY BERTRAM HODGES

ENLISTED in Royal Army Service Corps, M. T. Section, in May, 1915, and after serving a year in France, transferred to the Royal Fusiliers. Subsequently commissioned in the Manchester Regiment. Took part in engagements at Vimy Ridge and the Somme in 1916, and Messines, Ypres and Cambrai in 1917.

TRAVERS FREDERICK ORMSBY HOMAN

JOINED Dublin University O.T.C. in May, 1918, was promoted Lance-Corporal, and released after the Armistice.

STEPHEN ANDREW HUGGARD

ENLISTED in South Irish Horse in February, 1916, and transferred to 10th Batt. Royal Dublin Fusiliers in June following, and served in France until June, 1917. Commissioned in 11th Batt. Royal Dublin Fusiliers in January, 1918, and in May transferred to Royal Air Force, and qualified as Observer. Subsequently served in France and on the Rhine.

JOHN PURSER HUNTER

COMMISSIONED in Royal Army Service Corps in June, 1915, and served in England until November, 1916, when he was sent to Durban, South Africa. Subsequently appointed O.C., Embarkation Supply Depot, Margill, Mediterranean Expeditionary Force, promoted Captain, and mentioned in despatches. In March, 1919, appointed O.C., Garrison Supply Depot, Baghdad.

ARTHUR JAMES INGOLDSBY

JOINED Inns of Court O.T.C. in January, 1916, and was commissioned in 2/23rd Batt. London Regiment in January following. Served with Salonica Field Force from March to June, 1917, and with Egyptian Forces until June, 1918. Took part in operations in Palestine, and was wounded at Amman in March, 1918. Sent to France in June, 1918, and promoted Lieutenant in October. Promoted Captain, and awarded Military Cross :—
" For gallantry and devotion to duty. This officer led his Company with great dash and skill over very difficult ground. During the advance he became separated from his men owing to the mist and smoke of our barrage, and single-handed took many prisoners. Shortly afterwards he collected his men, who had become scattered, and rushed several machine gun positions, capturing many prisoners and five machine guns."

WILLIAM HENRY JEFFARES

COMMISSIONED Paymaster Sub-Lieut., Royal Naval Reserve, in July, 1915, and was subsequently promoted Paymaster-Lieutenant. Saw considerable service in the North Sea, and was present at the battle of Jutland.

JOHN PIM WATSON JOHNSTON

ENLISTED in 12th Batt. Royal Inniskilling Fusiliers in November, 1915, and was commissioned in the same Regiment in December, 1916. Sent to France in February, 1917, and took part in Messines attack in June, 1917. Was wounded at Ypres in following August. Was again sent to France in October, 1918, and took part in actions at Dadizeele, and crossings of the Lys and Scheldt. Subsequently posted to H.Q., 109th Infantry Brigade as Intelligence and Group Education Officer.

GEORGE DEAN JOHNSTON JONES

COMMISSIONED in 3rd Leinster Regt. in November, 1915 ; was sent to France early in 1916, and attached to 2nd Batt. Royal Irish Rifles. Took part in Somme offensive of that year, and was promoted Lieutenant in July, 1917. Wounded in the attack on Messines Ridge, was subsequently invalided home and took up light duty as R.T.O. Placed on retired list in March, 1918.

HAROLD VINCENT KEEGAN

ENLISTED in Royal Air Force in June, 1918, and being medically unfit, transferred to Royal Army Service Corps, M. T. Section. Served with North Russian Expeditionary Force from November, 1918, to September, 1919.

RICHARD BURNET PALMER KING

ENLISTED in South Irish Horse in September, 1914, and served for over a year as Motor Despatch Rider, Regimental H.Q. Sent to France in January, 1916, and took part in Somme offensive. Subsequently attached to 7th Batt. Royal Irish Regiment, and was appointed Lance-Corporal in charge of Lewis Gun Section in November, 1917. Taken prisoner near Lempire on 21st March, 1918, sent to Chemnitz, Saxony, and repatriated after the Armistice.

WILLIAM ELLIOTT MOTHERWELL KYLE

ENLISTED in Royal Air Force in October, 1918.

NORMAN PILFOLD LANGFORD

COMMISSIONED Sub-Lieut., Royal Naval Volunteer Reserve in June, 1918, and attached to H.M.S. " Hermione." Subsequently volunteered for hydrophone service, obtaining 1st Class Certificate, and served with Southern Patrol Force in the English Channel, and with Mine Clearance Service on East Coast of England.

STANLEY THOMAS CLIFFORD LANGFORD

JOINED Royal Air Force in May, 1918, and was promoted Flight Cadet, Naval Kite Balloon Section, in October following.

HUGH GRAHAM LATIMER

ENLISTED in 7th Batt. Royal Dublin Fusiliers (Pals) in September, 1914, and took part in the landing at Suvla Bay in August, 1915, and subsequent operations at Gallipoli. Subsequently invalided home owing to illness, and after serving with the 3rd and 10th Battalions Royal Dublin Fusiliers, he was discharged " Permanently unfit for Military Service."

WILLIAM LAWLESS

ENLISTED in Royal Army Medical Corps, and saw considerable service in France, and at Malta.

SAMUEL LE BAS

ENLISTED in 11th Batt. Royal Dublin Fusiliers in July, 1917, and transferred to Machine Gun Corps in following December. Sent to France in March, 1918, and took part in actions at Morlancourt, Le Cateau, Mormal Forest and Landrecies. Subsequently served with the Army of Occupation.

ERNEST GEORGE LEE

COMMISSIONED in 3rd Batt. Royal Irish Regiment in September, 1915, and took part in Somme offensive in June, 1916. Subsequently served with 182nd Trench Mortar Battery, and was promoted Lieutenant in March, 1917. Taken prisoner near St. Quentin in April, 1917, and spent over a year at Holyminden Camp, under the notorious Commandant, Niemeyer. Repatriated after the Armistice.

RICHARD FRANCIS LENANE

ENLISTED in 19th Hussars in September, 1914, and was transferred to 3rd Batt. Gloucestershire Regt. in June, 1915. Gazetted Sec. Lieutenant, 3rd Batt. Connaught Rangers, in September following; was sent to France in July, 1916, and attached to 2nd Batt. Royal Inniskilling Fusiliers, with which Batt. he served until demobilised. Mentioned in Sir Douglas Haig's despatches.

GEORGE ERNEST MALONE

JOINED Dublin University O.T.C. in May, 1918, and subsequently transferred to Royal Air Force.

JOHN DERMOTT MALONE

JOINED Dublin University O.T.C. in April, 1918, and subsequently transferred to Royal Air Force.

HORACE MAY

ENLISTED in South Irish Horse at outbreak of War, and was attached to the 16th (Irish) Division in France in 1915. Served in Loos, Hulloch, and Lens districts. Invalided out of the Army in September, 1917, owing to illness caused by exposure on active service.

WILLIAM MERCIER

ENLISTED in North Irish Horse in January, 1915, and was sent to France with the 34th Division as Sergeant in January, 1916. Took part in operations at the Somme, Arras, Ypres and Passchendaele. Gazetted to a Commission in the Royal Irish Fusiliers in October, 1918.

ALBERT CHARLES GORDON MEYERS

COMMISSIONED in Royal Army Service Corps in February, 1915, and promoted Captain in June, 1917. Sent to France in following October, and attached to 31st Divisional Train, with which he served until demobilised.

VICTOR GREEN MOLLOY

JOINED Dublin University O.T.C. in October, 1918, and was released after the Armistice.

ROBERT MONTEITH

JOINED Inns of Court O.T.C. in March, 1917, and gazetted Sec. Lieut., 12th Royal Irish Rifles, in following October. Wounded and taken prisoner on 21st March, 1918, and repatriated after the Armistice. Awarded Military Cross for operations during retreat of 21st March, 1918.

IRWIN WILLIAM MOORE

ENLISTED in 6th Royal Inniskilling Fusiliers in September, 1914, and was commissioned in 9th South Lancashire Regiment in April, 1915. Sent to France in following August, and attached to 1st York and Lancs. Regiment. Served at Kemmel and battle of Loos, and in December was sent to Egypt, and subsequently to Macedonia, where he took part in the advance on the Struma, and further operations in September, 1918. Afterwards posted to Army of Black Sea, and served in Turkey and Asia Minor. Twice mentioned in General Milne's despatches.

MICHAEL MORGAN

ARMY Reservist. Joined 41st Co. Royal Garrison Artillery in August, 1914, and was sent with Ammunition Column to France. Subsequently attached to a Siege Battery in Belgium for about two years, and acted as Bombardier.

FREDERICK WILLIAM MORRISON

COMMISSIONED in North Staffordshire Regiment in May, 1915, transferred to Machine Gun Corps in November following, and was shortly afterwards sent to France, where he lost left arm in July, 1916. Subsequently was employed as Adjutant of 2nd Reserve Batt. M. G. Corps, and was again sent to France as Staff-Lieut., G.H.Q. until demobilised.

THOMAS FRANCIS EDWIN MORROW

ENLISTED in 19th Batt. Royal Irish Rifles (Reserve) in November, 1916, and was attached to 9th Batt. in France in January, 1917. Promoted Lance-Corporal in following July, and took part in battles of Messines, Cambrai and Ypres. Promoted Corporal in December, 1917, and was gassed and taken prisoner on 21st March, 1918. Repatriated after the Armistice.

68

THOMAS JOSEPH MARY MURRAY

GAZETTED Sec. Lieut., Royal Army Service Corps, in June, 1915; attached to 39th Divisional Train, and promoted Lieutenant in September, 1915. Took part in Somme battle in 1916, and was promoted Captain in April, 1917. Mentioned in despatches in following month, and took part in battle of Ypres in July, and retreat of 5th Army from Peronne on 21st March, 1918. Subsequently served in the advance of the Canadian Corps from August, 1918, to the Armistice. Awarded Military Cross in June, 1918 :—" For distinguished services rendered in connection with military operations."

ALEXANDER McCAIG

JOINED Dublin University O.T. Corps in April, 1918, and was commissioned in Royal Inniskilling Fusiliers in following October.

HAMILTON McCLARTY

COMMISSIONED in 6th Batt. Royal Munster Fusiliers in September, 1914, and served for a lengthened period in France.

JOSEPH NORMAN McCLEANE

COMMISSIONED in 10th Batt. Royal Inniskilling Fusiliers in May, 1915, and served with the Ulster Division at Hebuterne. Invalided home in December, 1915, and after recovery, served with the 12th Battalion Royal Inniskilling Fusiliers at Enniskillen. Invalided out of the Army owing to ill-health in September, 1916.

JAMES NORMAN TOWNSEND McCONKEY

JOINED Inns of Court O.T. Corps in June, 1918, and was subsequently transferred to 5th King's Royal Rifle Corps.

THOMAS McDONALD

JOINED Artists Rifles O.T.C. in June, 1918.

GEORGE HERBERT McELNAY

GAZETTED Sec. Lieut., 3rd Batt. Royal Dublin Fusiliers in July, 1915, and attached to the 8th Battalion in France in following May. Wounded at the battle of the Somme in September, 1916, and after recovery was attached to the 7th Batt. in Palestine as Lieutenant. Returned to France in May, 1918, and was again wounded at Le Cateau in November, 1918. Awarded the Military Cross :—
" For conspicuous courage and ability. He took command of the firing line when all the senior officers had become casualties. He reorganised the line when the final objective had been taken, and made suitable arrangements, which defeated an enemy counter-attack on the right flank of the battalion."

JAMES McKELLAR

ENLISTED in King's Royal Rifle Corps in November, 1918.

JOHN McKENZIE

CALLED up to the Royal Dublin Fusiliers in November, 1916, and was transferred to the Army Pay Corps in the following February. He was appointed Acting-Paymaster in January, 1918, and was promoted to Senior Grade in August, 1918.

JOHN JAMES MacPHAIL

ENLISTED in South Irish Horse in November, 1915, and was sent to France in the following June. He was gassed at the battle of Arras in May, 1917, whilst engaged on Artillery observation with the 1st Corps Scouts, and was sent home medically unfit for overseas service.

JAMES McCABE NAPIER

ENLISTED in 18th Batt. Royal Irish Rifles in July, 1915, and was gazetted Sec. Lieut. in January, 1916. Transferred to 11th Batt., and sent to France in July following, and promoted Lieutenant in July, 1917. Took part in actions at Messines, Ypres, and Cambrai in 1917, and advance on Cambrai in 1918. Gassed in April, 1918, and wounded in the following October.

MARTIN WILLIAM NOLAN

GAZETTED Sec. Lieut., Loyal North Lancashire Regiment, in November, 1914, was sent to France in the following June, and served at Ypres and on the Somme. Was severely wounded near Loos in November, 1915. After recovery, was again sent to France, and took part in actions at Arras and Messines. Commanded a Company until July, 1917, and was again severely wounded. In November, 1917, passed permanently unfit for general service. Transferred to Royal Flying Corps in February, 1918, and was later appointed Flying Instructor.

CHARLES O'NEILL

ENLISTED in 7th Batt. Royal Dublin Fusiliers (Pals) in September, 1914 ; took part in the landing at Suvla Bay in the following August and was wounded in the right leg. After recovery, served with the 3rd Battalion, and with the 10th Battalion during the Rebellion. Sent to France as Corporal in July, 1916, and was later promoted Lance-Sergeant. Invalided home suffering from a severe gun-shot wound in the right arm, received at Beaumont Hamel in November, 1916, and was discharged unfit for further service in September, 1917.

HENRY GEORGE O'NEILL

JOINED Dublin University O.T.C. (Royal Field Artillery Unit) in April, 1918, and was released after the Armistice.

72

MICHAEL DILLON O'RORKE

ENLISTED in Irish Guards in September, 1914, and was commissioned in 3rd Batt. Connaught Rangers in April, 1915. In October, 1916, he was posted for service with the 1st Batt. Connaught Rangers on the Turco-Mesopotamian Front, and took part in the advance on Ramadi. Invalided home in June, 1918.

DUDLEY PERSSE

ENLISTED in Royal Army Service Corps in November, 1918, and served in England until demobilised.

GEORGE OWEN PEIRCE

COMMISSIONED in Royal Field Artillery (T.F.) in September, 1914 ; promoted Lieutenant in June, 1915, and Temporary Captain in October following. Acted as Gunnery Instructor until January, 1917, when he was posted to the 232nd Army Field Artillery Brigade in France as Lieutenant. Served at the battle of Arras in April, and Messines, Wytschaete Ridge and Ypres in July, 1917, and temporarily commanded his Battery. Wounded in action, and awarded the Military Cross, and subsequently took part in engagements at Passchendaele and Cambrai, and in the retreat of March, 1918. Was later promoted Major, and served in Germany. Awarded Military Cross :—" For devotion to duty, and bravery in the field. During the absence of the Commander, he commanded the battery with great skill and effect, and on another occasion, under intense hostile fire, at great personal risk, succeeded in rescuing two men from a burning gun-pit."

ROBERT VICTOR POLLEY

COMMISSIONED in Royal Irish Fusiliers in November, 1915 ; sent to France in the following July, and served with the 11th Entrenching Battalion and 8th Royal Inniskilling Fusiliers. Took part in battles of Somme, 1916, Messines Ridge, and Passchendaele in 1917, and was twice wounded. Promoted Lieutenant in February, and mentioned in despatches. Attached to Ministry of Labour in June, 1918.

JOHN JAMES McELNAY POLLOCK

ENLISTED in 7th Batt. Leinster Regiment in July, 1915 ; was sent to France in following December, and served at La Bassée, Hulloch, Loos, and on the Somme. Wounded at Guillemont in September, 1916 ; and after recovery was commissioned in 9th Royal Irish Fusiliers. Took part in Cambrai attack in November, 1917 ; was taken prisoner in March, 1918, and repatriated after the Armistice.

CLAUDE ALEXANDER POLSON

ENLISTED in South Irish Horse in September, 1914 ; was sent to France in December, 1915, and invalided to Netley Hospital in the following April, suffering from blood-poisoning. Discharged unfit for further military service in March, 1917.

GEORGE CECIL POLSON

ENLISTED in South Irish Horse in October, 1915, and was subsequently commissioned in 4th Batt. Royal Irish Regiment. Sent to France in December, 1916; took part in battles of Messines and Wytschaete in June, 1917, and was severely wounded at Ypres in July following. Placed on retired list in July, 1918, on account of ill-health caused by wounds.

JOHN POWER

ENLISTED in Royal Garrison Artillery at the outbreak of War, and was shortly afterwards invalided out of the service.

JOHN HOPKINS PRATT

JOINED Dublin University O.T.C. in November, 1915, and was commissioned in 3rd Batt. Royal Inniskilling Fusiliers in January, 1916. Attached to the 2nd Battalion in France in the following July; promoted Lieutenant, and took part in the Somme operations of 1916, and in actions at St. Quentin, Nieuport, and Ypres in 1917. Transferred to the Tank Corps in January, 1918.

HENRY DE LACHEROIS PURDON

ENLISTED in South Irish Horse in September, 1914 ; was sent to France in April following, and served with the 49th Division, then in the line south of Armentieres. In June, 1916, was transferred to the Military Mounted Police. Mentioned in despatches.

CLIFFORD LAW REARDON

COMMISSIONED Paymaster Sub-Lieutenant R.N.R. in June, 1916, and served in North Sea on patrol duty. In August, 1917, appointed to H.M.S. "Jonquil," then employed on escort duty in the Mediterranean. Promoted Paymaster Lieutenant in May, 1918.

ALBERT EDWARD SANDWITH ROOKE

ENLISTED in Royal Army Service Corps in May, 1918, and was released after the Armistice.

RICHARD THOMAS ROSS

ENLISTED in Royal Army Service Corps in May, 1915, and was sent to France with the 38th Welsh Division in the following November as Staff-Sergt.-Major. Served at Havre, Rouen, Calais, and in the Arras Sector, and was posted Group Officer at Boulogne in September, 1917. Sent to Italy in October following, and after serving a year in that country, was sent home for a Commission. Gazetted Sec. Lieutenant in February, 1919.

THOMAS ROTHWELL

JOINED Inns of Court O.T.C. in February, 1916;
commissioned Sec. Lieut., Royal Dublin Fusiliers,
in December following, and was attached to 9th
Batt. in France in February, 1917. Took part in
operations at Messines Ridge in June, 1916; was
wounded and awarded M.C. Subsequently attached
to 6th Battalion in Egypt and Palestine, and on
returning to France, served in the Mormal Forest
operations, leading up to the Armistice. Awarded
Military Cross :—" For conspicuous gallantry and
devotion to duty. Although wounded early in the
attack, he led his Company with great pluck and
skill, and having gained his objective, set vigorously
to work upon the consolidation. Although much
exhausted by his serious wound, he would not
avail himself of medical aid until urged to do so
by his commanding officer. He set a splendid
example of devotion to duty."

LESLIE CAMPBELL RUTTLEDGE

COMMISSIONED Sub-Lieut., Royal Naval Volunteer
Reserve, in July, 1917, and after taking out Gunnery
Certificate, joined H.M.S. " Diadem." Subsequently
transferred to Auxiliary Patrol Service, and was
attached to Motor Launch Section in the Adriatic,
operating against hostile submarines. Later sent
to Mudros, and placed in temporary command
for mine-clearing service. Subsequently promoted
Lieutenant.

WILLIAM GEORGE STEPHENS SEARIGHT

ENLISTED in Honorable Artillery Company in May,
1915, and was sent overseas in following autumn.
Took part in engagements near Aden, and transferred to Egypt, Canal Defences, in January, 1916.
Served in battles of Romani, Raffa, El Arish,
Gaza, and Palestine offensive, culminating in capture
of Beersheba and Jaffa. Later took part in capture
of Jerusalem and Jericho. In the spring of 1918,
joined Royal Flying Corps, and was gazetted Flying
Officer in the following June. Subsequently placed
on Home Establishment.

EDMOND SHEEHAN

ENLISTED in 5th Royal Irish Regiment in August,
1914, and took part in the landing at Suvla Bay
in August, 1915. Subsequently promoted Sergeant,
and served in Serbia until August, 1917. Sent to
Palestine, and took part in the advance on Beersheba, and in the operations at Jerusalem.
Transferred to France in March, 1918, and served
in the advance of that year.

GEORGE HENRY SHERIDAN

COMMISSIONED Sec. Lieut., Royal Irish Rifles, in
November, 1915, and in the following October was
sent to France, where he served until May, 1917,
when he was invalided home.

T. SHERIDAN.

ARMY Reservist. Called up at outbreak of War, and was sent to France in August, 1914, with 1st Batt. Connaught Rangers. Wounded in the leg at Hill 60, and after recovery, was again sent to France, and severely wounded in the arm. Subsequently promoted Sergeant, and employed training men at various Depots.

THOMAS ALEXANDER SHERIDAN

ENLISTED in 19th Reserve Batt., Royal Irish Rifles, in April, 1916, and was sent to France in the autumn of the following year. Took part in engagements at Messines, Ypres, and Cambrai in 1917. Transferred to 15th Batt. R. I. Rifles in March, 1918, and was severely wounded in Flanders offensive in August following, necessitating amputation of right leg.

NICHOLAS JOHN SINGLETON

ARMY Reservist, 5th Royal Irish Lancers. Rejoined colours on 6th August, 1914 ; sent to France on 15th of that month, and took part in the battle of Mons and retreat from Mons, and at the Aisne and Marne in September, 1914. Subsequently served at 1st and 2nd battles of Ypres, Neuve Chapelle and Loos, the Somme, Arras, Cambrai, and was mentioned in despatches for work at the defence of Amiens in March, 1918. Later took part in the advance of 1918, having served " from Mons to Mons," as his Regiment entered that town on the morning of 11th November, 1918, when hostilities ceased.

ALBERT MAUNSELL SMITH

ENLISTED in 7th Royal Dublin Fusiliers in September, 1914, and was commissioned in 5th Royal Irish Fusiliers in following December. Served in Serbia in 1915, and was invalided through illness. After recovery, served in Egypt, and in May, 1916, was promoted Staff Lieutenant. Sent to Palestine in 1918, where he served until the defeat of the Germano Turkish forces. Promoted Captain 1st May, 1918.

GEORGE THOMAS STOKES

JOINED Royal Army Service Corps, M.T. Section, in May, 1918, and was transferred to 1st Reserve Garrison Battalion Suffolk Regiment in following September, and to 3rd Batt. in October.

ARTHUR SULLIVAN

ENLISTED in 7th Batt. Leinster Regiment in July, 1915, and was gazetted Sec. Lieut., 15th Batt. Liverpool Regiment, in following December. In July, 1918, was attached to 22nd Batt. Northumberland Fusiliers, with which battalion he served on La Bassée sector until December, 1918.

THOMAS HAMILTON SULLIVAN

ENLISTED in 17th (Res.) Battalion Royal Irish Rifles in June, 1915, and was employed as Musketry Instructor until early in 1916. Commissioned in 1917, and was attached to 13th Batt. Royal Irish Rifles at Messines. Took part in engagements at Passchendaele Ridge and Cambrai in 1917, and was wounded near Rozieres in German offensive of March, 1918. Subsequently promoted Lieutenant.

HENRY DOUGLAS SWAYNE

ENLISTED in Royal Engineers, Motor Cyclist Despatch Rider, in February, 1915 ; was sent to France in following September, and took part in the battle of the Somme in 1916. Commissioned in Royal Irish Rifles in September, 1917 ; sent to France in the following November, and was slightly gassed and taken prisoner at St. Quentin in March, 1918. Repatriated after the Armistice, and subsequently promoted Lieutenant.

SAMUEL GEORGE SWITZER

COMMISSIONED in Army Pay Corps in February, 1916, and being medically unfit for service overseas, served at Cork Barracks.

WELDON JOHN TARLETON

ENLISTED in North Irish Horse in August, 1915, and, on being sent to France, was posted to Divisional Cavalry to 51st Highland Division. Invalided in 1916 with trench fever, and being passed unfit for further service overseas, he acted as Clerk to the Military Convalescent Hospital, Holywood.

ROBERT JAMES TATE

JOINED Dublin University O.T.C. in May, 1918, and transferred to Royal Air Force in following August.

ALFRED EDWARD TEGART

COMMISSIONED Sec. Lieut., Royal Army Service Corps, in September, 1914. Served in France, and was promoted Captain.

DAVID WALTER LANGFORD THORPE

JOINED Inns of Court O.T.C. in January, 1917, and was gazetted Sec. Lieut., Royal Field Artillery, in February, 1918. Served in France and Belgium, and with the Army of Occupation in Germany.

ROBERT HODDER TWIGG

ENLISTED in 18th Batt. Royal Fusiliers (Public
Schools) in May, 1915, and was sent to France in
following November.   Commissioned in Leinster
Regiment in September, 1916, and served with
the 1st Batt. in the Struma Valley.   Subsequently
sent to Egypt, and took part in operations at
Beersheba and Judean Hills, and in the attack on
Furkhah Ridge, in September, 1918, when the
Turkish line was finally broken at one of
its strongest points.

EDWARD VICTOR TWISS

Gazetted Sec. Lieut., Royal Munster Fusiliers, in
July, 1915, and was attached to 2nd Batt. in France
in May, 1916.   Took part in actions at Contal-
maison, Pozieres, and High Wood in the Somme
movement in 1916.   Mentioned in despatches for
work at the crossing of the Somme at Brie in
March, 1917.   Subsequently trained for the
landing at Zeebrugge, and served with the Canadian
Corps at Passchendaele in November, 1917, when
he was again mentioned in despatches.   Later
attached to 2/1 West Kent Yeomanry for home
service.

GEORGE FRANCIS VAN MAANEN

ENLISTED in North Irish Horse in November, 1916, and was posted to 1st Battalion in France in following March, and served on the Arras front and in Belgium. Subsequently attached to 1/4th South Lancashire Regiment at Ypres. Contracted blood poisoning, and was invalided home in August, 1917, and was afterwards promoted Sergeant in North Irish Horse.

CHARLES DOUGLAS WADDELL

ENLISTED in 14th Batt. Royal Irish Rifles in September, 1914, and was commissioned in following January. Sent to France in October, 1915, and attached to a Trench Mortar Battery. Awarded Military Cross for work at Thiepval Wood in July, 1916. Invalided home with shell-shock in June, 1917, and was subsequently appointed O.C., Trench Mortar Battery, Dublin District. Promoted Captain in May, 1918.

ANDREW ERNEST WALKER

GAZETTED Sec. Lieut., 6th Royal Dublin Fusiliers, in September, 1915 ; was subsequently transferred to 10th Batt. Royal Irish Rifles, and served in France until October, 1916, when he was invalided home with trench fever. Later promoted Lieut., and appointed Instructor, Northern School of Signalling.

EDWARD KENNEDY WALKINGTON

ENLISTED in Royal Fusiliers (Public Schools) in September, 1914, and was gazetted 2nd Lieut. in 3rd Batt. Royal Irish Fusiliers. Sent to France in May, 1916, and was wounded at Ginchy in September following. Again sent to France in May, 1918, and wounded near Bailleul in August, 1918. Subsequently gazetted to a Commission in the Regular Army.

WILLIAM HAVILAND WATERS

JOINED Inns of Court O.T.C. in June, 1915 and was commissioned in 4th Batt. Royal Irish Fusiliers in October, 1915. Subsequently sent to France, and transferred to Indian Army in July, 1918. Awarded M.C. :—" For conspicuous gallantry and devotion to duty. He showed splendid leadership and courage when one of the companies had lost most of its officers and N.C.O.'s in an attack. He organised an attack on a point which was causing heavy casualties and captured it, putting the whole garrison out of action and capturing a machine-gun and some prisoners."

JOHN GUSTAVUS FENTON WHEATLEY

ENLISTED in Royal Engineers as Motor Cycle Despatch Rider in May, 1916, and was sent to France in following September. Served at the battle of the Somme in 1916, and later at Arras and Ypres.

RONALD PARKE WHEATLEY

ENLISTED in Royal Army Service Corps, M.T. Section, in May, 1918; was sent to France in the following July, and served on the Belgian front until the Armistice.

HENRY VERE WHITE

COMMISSIONED in Royal Army Service Corps in September, 1914, and was sent to France with 6th Division in following November. Promoted Lieutenant in March, 1915, and Captain in the following October, and was mentioned in despatches in November, 1918. Subsequently served with the Midland Division, Army of Occupation.

THOMAS HENRY WHITE

GAZETTED Sec. Lieut., 19th Royal Irish Rifles, in February, 1916; was sent to France in June, and took part in Somme offensive in July following. Wounded in May, 1917, and again severely wounded at 3rd battle of Ypres in August, and invalided home. Again sent to France as Lieutenant in May, 1918, and attached to 7/8th Royal Inniskilling Fusiliers, and slightly wounded in August near Kemmel. Retransferred to 19th Royal Irish Rifles in September, 1918, and took part in capture of Neuve Eglise, and Courtrai, and crossing of the Lys.

GEORGE ALBERT WIGGINS

ENLISTED in Royal Field Artillery in September, 1916 ; was sent to France in May, 1917, and served at Avrincourt, Ypres, Nieuport and Festubert, and also at Bucquoy in the retreat in March, 1918.

WILLIAM FREDERIC WILLIAMS

ENLISTED in Royal Field Artillery in May, 1918, and was posted at 7th Reserve Brigade, Signal Section.

WILLIAM THOMAS WILLIAMSON

JOINED Dublin University O.T.C. in May, 1918, and was released after the Armistice.

REGINALD PERCY WISDOM

JOINED Artists Rifles O.T.C. in July, 1918.

DECORATIONS AND HONOURS

Distinguished Service Order :

MAJOR W. N. FOSTER.

O.B.E. :

MAJOR G. W. FRAZER.

M.B.E. :

PAYMASTER LIEUT. J. M. DIVER.

Military Cross :

MAJOR G. O. PEIRCE.
CAPTAIN E. J. BRETT.
CAPTAIN A. J. INGOLDSBY.
CAPTAIN T. J. M. MURRAY.
CAPTAIN C. D. WADDELL.
LIEUT. P. C. BELL.
LIEUT. W. H. WATERS.
SEC. LIEUT. G. U. CASHEL.
SEC. LIEUT. ROBT. MONTEITH.
SEC. LIEUT. G. H. McELNAY.
SEC. LIEUT. T. ROTHWELL.

Mentioned in Despatches :

MAJOR W. N. FOSTER.

MAJOR R. R. CUSACK.

CAPTAIN A. ATHERTON.

CAPTAIN E. J. BRETT.

CAPTAIN C. D. HARVEY.

CAPTAIN J. P. HUNTER.

CAPTAIN T. J. M. MURRAY.

CAPTAIN H. V. WHITE.

LIEUT. R. F. LENANE.

LIEUT. I. W. MOORE.

LIEUT. R. V. POLLEY.

LIEUT. E. V. TWISS.

SERGT. J. S. GIBSON.

BDR. R. W. COURTNEY.

CORPL. F. W. HALL.

CORPL. H. DE L. PURDON.

CORPL. N. J. SINGLETON.

Military Medal :

SERGT. G. H. FRAZER.

Meritorious Service Medal :

Q.-M.-SERGT. J. H. DORRITTY.

SERGT. G. O'H. BEVERIDGE.

Parchment Certificates for Gallantry :

LIEUT. E. R. GRAY.

SEC. LIEUT. (ACTG.-CAPT.) D. N. KARNEY (Killed).

SEC. LIEUT. C. L. HENRY (Killed).

SERGT. J. W. GIFFORD.

FOREIGN DECORATIONS.

Order of the Nile—4th Class :

CAPTAIN C. D. HARVEY.   LIEUT. J. ACHESON.

TABLE.

Number of Officials	Enlisted, etc. ..		..	190
				——
Do.	Killed in Action	16		
Do.	Died of Wounds	8		
Do.	Died on Service, etc.	7		
Do.	Missing ..	2		
		——		33
Do.	Returned to Bank		..	122
Do.	Who took up other employment		..	35
				——
				190
				——
Do.	Wounded ..		..	47

www.ingramcontent.com/pod-product-compliance
Lightning Source LLC
Chambersburg PA
CBHW070944150426
42812CB00066B/3259/J